UNCOVERING THE PAST

THE COLD WAR AND THE CUBAN MISSILE CRISIS

NATALIE HYDE

Crabtree Publishing Company

www.crabtreebooks.com

Author: Natalie Hyde
Publishing plan research and development:
  Reagan Miller
Editor-in-chief: Lionel Bender
Editors: Simon Adams, Anastasia Suen,
  Lynn Peppas
Proofreaders: Laura Booth, Petrice Custance
Project coordinator: Kathy Middleton
Design and photo research: Ben White
Cover design: Ken Wright
Production coordinator and
  Prepress technician: Samara Parent
Print coordinator: Margaret Amy Salter
Production coordinated by:
  Bender Richardson White

Consultant: Amie Wright, The New York
  Public Library

Photographs and reproductions:
Photographs: Library of Congress: cover; Corbis: 14 top Rt (Lebrecht Authors/Lebrecht Music & Arts); Getty 15 (Robert W. Kelley/The LIFE Premium Collection), 30 (AFP), 38–39 (U.S. Navy), 40-41 (Jung Yeon-Je), 41 bottom right (Jung Yeon-Je); Shutterstock: 1 (Anibal Trejo), 3 (bernd.neeser), 4, 6 Icon (KKulikov), 8, 10, 12, 14 Icon (Everett Historical), 16, 18, 20, 22 Icon (Sergey Kamshylin), 24, 26, 28, 31 Icon (Niyazz) 32, 34, 36, Icon (John Wollwerth), 36 (Mario Savoia), 38, 40 Icon (Foto011); Topfoto: 4–5 (The Granger Collection), 6, 7 (The Granger Collection), 8-9 (Ullsteinbild), 10–11 (Ullsteinbild), 11 (The Granger Collection), 12 (The Granger Collection), 13, 17 (Topham Picturepoint), 18 (The Granger Collection), 19 (The Granger Collection), 20-21 (The Granger Collection), 22 (World History Archive), 23 (Topham Picturepoint), 24 (The Granger Collection), 25 (Ronald Grant Archive), 26 (Topham Picturepoint), 27 (Fine Art Images/HIP), 28 (The Granger Collection), 29, 30 (ullsteinbild), 32–33 (Topham Picturepoint), 34 (ullsteinbild), 35 (The Granger Collection), 37 (The Granger Collection).
Graphics: Stefan Chabluk

Cover photo: Students hide under desks during a "take cover" drill practice in Brooklyn, New York, 1962.

Library and Archives Canada Cataloguing in Publication

Hyde, Natalie, 1963-, author
    The Cold War and the Cuban Missle Crisis / Natalie Hyde.

(Uncovering the past: analyzing primary sources)
Includes bibliographical references and index.
Issued in print and electronic formats.
ISBN 978-0-7787-2570-1 (bound).--ISBN 978-0-7787-2572-5 (paperback).--
ISBN 978-1-4271-1760-1 (html)

    1. Cold War--Sources--Juvenile literature. 2. Cuban Missile Crisis,
1962--Sources--Juvenile literature. I. Title.

D843.H94 2016   j909.82'5   C2015-907982-9
                                          C2015-907983-7

Library of Congress Cataloguing in Publication

CIP available at Library of Congress

Crabtree Publishing Company

Printed in Canada/022016/MA20151130

www.crabtreebooks.com   1-800-387-7650

Published in Canada
Crabtree Publishing
616 Welland Ave.
St. Catharines, Ontario
L2M 5V6

Published in the
United States
Crabtree Publishing
PMB 59051
350 Fifth Avenue, 59th Floor
New York, NY 10118

Published in the
United Kingdom
Crabtree Publishing
Maritine House
Basin Road North, Hove
BN4 1WR

Published in Australia
Crabtree Publishing
3 Charles Street
Coburg North
VIC 3058

UNCOVERING THE PAST

INTRODUCTION: THE PAST COMES ALIVE................................4
    An introduction to the Cold War and the Cuban Missile
    Crisis and how we can use these events to learn about
    our history; the importance of studying history.

HISTORICAL SOURCES: TYPES OF EVIDENCE..........................8
    The three main types of primary sources of
    information: written, visual, and auditory;
    the use of secondary sources.

ANALYZING EVIDENCE: INTERPRETATION............................16
    The importance of analyzing primary sources
    and the dangers of bias; understanding context
    when analyzing source materials.

THE STORY UNCOVERED: THE COLD WAR............................20
    The history of the Cold War, political differences, wars
    by proxy, and superpower rivalry; the Cuban Missile
    Crisis and its resolution.

EVIDENCE REVISITED: DIFFERENT VIEWS............................32
    The evidence about the Cold War and the Cuban
    Missile Crisis and the different views it expresses; how
    people in different countries reacted.

MODERN EXAMPLES: HISTORY REPEATED............................38
    The new Cold War between Russia and the West over
    Ukraine and elsewhere; the continuing standoff
    between North and South Korea.

Timeline...42
Bibliography...44
Internet Guidelines..45
Glossary...46
Index 48

THE PAST COMES ALIVE

"Life can only be understood backwards; but it must be lived forwards."

Søren Kierkegaard, Danish philosopher, 1843

The **Cold War** was unlike any other conflict in history. It was a time of great fear and uncertainty. The United States of America and the Soviet Union threatened each other with weapons so powerful that the future of the entire world was at risk. The struggle came to a head with an event known as the Cuban Missile Crisis. The world held its breath as the leaders of the two countries tried to reach an agreement. Everyone hoped the world would never again come so close to destruction.

How can we prevent this from happening again? We can study the past. Things that have just happened are called the recent past. Things that happened long, long ago are the distant past. We often don't see things clearly as they are taking place. It is only after time has passed that we can look back at an event and understand how and why things happened. Important events show us the truth about people, their **cultures**, and their **beliefs**. We learn what works in **society** and what does not. We understand what causes people or society to change. When we learn about others, we learn about ourselves.

The Cold War had a huge **impact** on the world. It led to new **treaties** on **nuclear weapons**. It changed how leaders communicated. We saw how close the human race could come to destroying itself.

▶ These 1965 U.S. Nike anti-aircraft guided missiles were on mobile launchers and trailers so they could easily be moved. Crews manned them around the clock and lived in temporary huts nearby.

DEFINITIONS

We use different words to define time gone by:
A **decade** is a period of ten years, a **century** 100 years, and a **millennium** 1,000 years.
A **generation** is all the people born and living at the same time, such as millennials (those born from 1980 to the early 2000s).
An **era** is a period of time with a certain characteristic, such as the Cold War (1946–1991).
An **age** is a long period of time, such as the Atomic Age (after 1945).

EVIDENCE RECORD CARD

U.S. Army missiles
LEVEL Primary source
MATERIAL Black-and-white photograph
LOCATION Secret, in U.S.
DATE 1965
SOURCE Topfoto Agency

HOW DO WE LEARN ABOUT HISTORY?

There are many different ways to learn about our **history**. One way is to research a time period is by studying writings or images from that era. We can look in libraries, museums, or private collections. Information might be in newspapers, magazines, photograph albums, books, or scrapbooks. We can ask other people for information, too. Sometimes there are interviews or reports by people that were involved in or witnessed an event. These are called **firsthand** accounts. A report made by someone else who may have known someone who was there are called **secondhand** accounts.

A **historian** is someone who studies history. Often historians become an expert in one particular era or age. They might focus on one area of the world or on one special event. John Lewis Gaddis is a historian who has spent most of his career studying the

◀ On October 23, 1962, President John F. Kennedy signed a document banning the Soviets from delivering more weapons to Cuba. This photograph is held in the Library of Congress. It is the largest library in the world and holds millions of photographs, books, recordings, and maps.

ANALYZE THIS

Look at the setting for this photo. Where is Kennedy signing this document? What is he wearing? What expression is on his face? What impression do you get about this event based on what you see?

"It shall be the policy of this nation to regard any nuclear missile launched from Cuba against any nation in the Western Hemisphere as an attack on the United States, requiring a full retaliatory response upon the Soviet Union."

President Kennedy addressing the American people on television, October 22, 1962

Cold War. Historians have an important job. They find and collect information and make it available to others. They can help explain the causes or effects of events. Being a historian can also be a difficult job. Information can be hard to find, hard to read, or hard to understand.

Because the Cold War was a fairly **recent** event, there is a lot of material to study. The people involved may still be alive. **Documents** from the time are still available. The Cold War was of interest to the whole world, so many different **viewpoints** exist. It also happened at a time when we had the **technology**, such as cameras, recording devices, and movie cameras, to capture it.

There are also problems for historians researching the Cold War and the Cuban Missile Crisis. It was a highly **sensitive** event, so some **files** were kept secret by the governments. In addition, the viewpoints in articles and reports are different based on which country the material belongs to.

ANALYZE THIS

If you were researching the Cold War, where would be the best places to look for material? What problems could you run into?

▼ Newspapers reported the launch of the Russian satellite *Sputnik* in 1957. It signaled the beginning of the race to be the first country to send a human into space.

TYPES OF EVIDENCE

"What is all knowledge except recorded experience, and a product of history?"

Thomas Carlyle, Scottish historian, 1838

Anything created in the past that gives us information is called **source material**. Source material can be the documents and images found in libraries, museums, and private collections. It can also be found in an archive. An **archive** is a place that stores a mass of historical information about a location, a person, or an event.

Source material is an important part of understanding historical events. By studying items from the past we have the ability to come to our own conclusions about something instead of just reading someone else's opinion.

Sources can be very **fragile**. If they are not stored properly or if they are used a lot, they can become damaged. They need to be **preserved** so they will last. Historians might wear gloves to look at old books or papers. This is so the natural oils on our skin don't ruin the paper. Old newspapers can be **brittle**. Archives and libraries often take pictures or microfilm of old newspapers so that researchers can still see the information without damaging the original pages. Copies are sometimes made of old photographs so that the originals can be kept safe. **Artifacts** can be put in special cases that control the light and temperature to slow down aging. Today, **digital** images and copies of audio recordings can be preserved in computer files.

▲ This image shows West German citizens looking over the newly built Berlin Wall in 1961. This wall would divide friends and neighbors that used to live side by side.

PRIMARY SOURCES

There are two types of source material: **primary sources** and **secondary sources**. Primary sources are direct evidence or firsthand accounts of an event. Primary sources can be written, visual, or **auditory**.

Written primary sources can be:

- Diaries: Personal thoughts kept in a notebook
- Journals: Details of special events or trips in daily life
- Advertisements: Descriptions of items or services offered for sale
- Transcripts: Written copies of interviews, meetings, or speeches

▼ **Photographs are an important primary source. This photograph shows Checkpoint Charlie, a major crossing point through the Berlin Wall between East and West Berlin during the Cold War.**

ANALYZE THIS

Primary source material for the Cold War is found in many different countries. Why is it important to look at all source documents, and not just the sources from one area?

- Letters: Mail on paper sent between two people
- Telegrams: Messages sent by signals over a wire and then written down
- Lyrics: The words of a song
- Blogs: Journals posted online
- Social media: Posts and updates on social sites online

There is a great deal of primary source material for the Cold War and the Cuban Missile Crisis. This is due in part because the governments of the two nations were involved. The two governments kept records of all their meetings, documents, memorandums, and telegrams. The leaders sometimes kept their own personal papers about the events, such as the Soviet Union's leader, Nikita Khrushchev. In later life, he wrote his **memoirs**, which is a book written by someone about their own personal life and career. In it, Khrushchev talks about his dealings with the United States during the Cuban Missile Crisis.

The militaries of both countries also kept records. There are military reports, **surveillance** photographs, and maps. Behind the scenes, **spy** agencies, such as the Central Intelligence Agency (CIA) in the United States and the KGB in the Soviet Union, were also carefully following events and collecting information.

The outcome of the Cold War was important to all countries around the world. Every move was carefully watched and commented on by international newspapers, magazines, and television reporters. This left a large paper and photograph **trail**.

◄ This political cartoon shows the problems between the Western powers and the Soviet Union after World War II. Supplies to West Berlin were being choked off by the Soviets, represented by the bear. The artist, D. R. Fitzpatrick, created the cartoon in 1948. He went on to win several awards for his work.

"I would submit the proposition that any air strike must be directed not solely against the missile sites, but against the missile sites plus the airfields plus the aircraft which may not be on the airfields but hidden by that time plus all potential nuclear storage sites."

Excerpt from a transcript of the conversation between Robert McNamara, U.S. Secretary of Defense, with President John Kennedy, October 16, 1962

VISUAL SOURCES

Visual primary sources play an important part in our understanding of events. Photographs, paintings, and movies deliver a lot of information. Artwork created by a person not present at the time of an event is a secondary source, even if the artist was inspired by studying a primary source. A photograph taken during a particular time in the past is a primary source. But a photograph taken afterward —even of the same scene— is a secondary source.

Some primary visual evidence can be:

■ Photographs: Images created on film and printed on paper
■ Maps: Diagrams of a region or area
■ Posters: Images printed on large sheets of paper with or without words
■ Political cartoons: Images drawn by an illustrator to make a point, with or without words
■ Videos: Moving images recorded by a camera

▶ In this poster, the word for "No!" shows that the Russian people were just as afraid of nuclear destruction as other people around the world.

EVIDENCE RECORD CARD

Soviet anti-nuclear poster
LEVEL Primary source
MATERIAL Color poster
ARTIST Albert Aslyan
DATE 1958
SOURCE Topfoto

- Billboards: Large outdoor boards showing advertisements
- Flyers and brochures: Small **pamphlets** with information about services or products
- Paintings: Images made on canvas with paint

Photographs, maps, and political cartoons are the most common visual primary sources for the Cold War and the Cuban Missile Crisis. The military used **aerial** photographs and maps to pinpoint where weapons and troops might be. Newspaper photographers captured important moments between the leaders of the United States and the Soviet Union. Video footage preserves television addresses and speeches.

Information that we can hear is called auditory source material, such as music or recordings of interviews, speeches, or news reports. Auditory sources give us details of an event, but they can also provide an understanding of the emotions of those involved. You can hear fear in a person's voice. The sounds of sirens, explosions, crowds chanting, or people crying give a clear picture of the impact on lives. During the Cold War and Cuban Missile Crisis the government made recordings of telephone conversations, radio and TV addresses, and even meetings. There are many interviews with officials and news reports as the conflict reached its peak.

ARTIFACTS AS PRIMARY EVIDENCE

Artifacts are items made by people. They can also be primary sources. Some Cold War artifacts include nuclear attack survival kits, pieces of the Berlin Wall, flags of communist countries, and "spy" gadgets, such as shoes with secret weapons and coins with hidden blades. These items remind us of how events affect the lives of the people involved.

▼ This aerial photograph taken off the coast of Cuba shows part of a load of 15 IL-28 bombers aboard the Soviet ship *Kasimov* on December 9, 1962.

SECONDARY SOURCES

Secondary sources are one step farther away from the actual event. These materials are created by studying, talking about, or **evaluating** information found in primary sources.

Some secondary sources are:
- Novels: Stories that are fictional
- Textbooks: Books containing facts and figures
- Magazine articles: Writing that focuses on a topic
- Encyclopedias: A set of books that give a little information on many subjects
- Movies: Fictional stories on film

Several novels are set during the Cold War. One of the most famous is *The Spy Who Came In From The Cold* by John le Carré. It takes place in East Germany, the part that was controlled by the Soviet Union. It became an international hit because it showed that spies on both sides could be **dishonorable**.

From Russia With Love is a well-known James Bond film based on a book of the same name. The background of the story was the tension between the United States and the Soviet Union. Like the Cold War, two spy agencies in the book are fighting for control of the world.

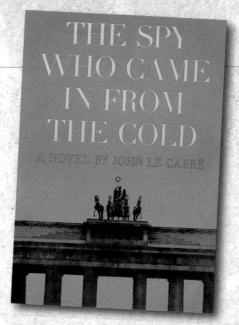

▲ The book *The Spy Who Came In From The Cold* takes place in East Berlin but the movie was actually shot in England and Ireland. Great efforts were made to make the movie accurate in every detail.

Even children's stories can be set during the Cold War. *The Calculus Affair* is an episode of the Tintin comic series. The story centers around the invention of a machine capable of destroying anything with sound waves. The idea of mass destruction shows the thinking of the time when everyone was concerned with nuclear weapons and the end of the world.

Secondary source material is a good way to understand how events can affect people. It lets us reflect on how world events change ordinary people's lives.

"There was only one light in the checkpoint, a reading lamp with a green shade, but the glow of the arclights, like artificial moonlight, filled the cabin. Darkness had fallen, and with it silence. They spoke as if they were afraid of being overheard."

John le Carré, from *The Spy Who Came In From The Cold*, 1963

LIFE

THE DANGER-FILLED WEEK OF DECISION

CUBA

IN BRILLIANT COLOR
The Great Council in Rome

U.S. NAVY
OFF CUBA

NOVEMBER 2 · 1962 · 20¢

▲ This cover of *Life* magazine shows U.S. Navy warships and planes off the coast of Cuba. The articles inside are secondary sources because they are the ideas and thoughts of the authors. The pictures and diagrams illustrating the articles are all primary sources.

INTERPRETATION

*"History is truly the witness of times past,
the light of truth."*

Cicero, Roman philosopher, 55 B.C.E.

Historians study and write about history. They look for facts and details in source material to help them understand people and events in the past. But not everything that is written gives true information. Som▮▮▮▮s the way people present information is **colored** by their background, beliefs, or experiences. They may show that they are in favor or against a thing, person, or group compared to others. This imbalanced view is called **bias**.

Historians deal with bias by always being aware of where or by whom the information was created. They use something known as the Bias Rule when evaluating source material.

The Bias Rule states that:

- Every piece of source material must be studied carefully
- The view of the person who created it must be considered
- All source material should be compared with other pieces of information

The Cold War was fought between two very different countries. The governments had opposite vie▮▮▮ how a country should be run. The information on what was happening during the Cold War is biased depending on the source of the information. Soviet newspapers felt their military was protecting Russian interests. Posters, articles, and speeches show this point of view. American leaders saw the Soviets as a threat. American magazines, newspapers, and TV news shows reported from the view that the Americans were preventing **injustice** and preserving their way of life.

▶ American news media showed images of Cubans who were working against their leader, Fidel Castro. Here anti-Castro forces are studying maps just before the planned invasion of Cuba.

PERSPECTIVES

Look at this image of anti-Castro forces. Do they look ready and confident in their task? How do you think Russian citizens would feel if they saw this in a newspaper? How would Americans feel?

ANALYZING SOURCE MATERIAL

The more care historians take in **analyzing** source material, the better information they will get. They not only look for bias, but they also look for other signs of how true and **accurate** the source may be.

Historians use the Time and Place Rule when analyzing sources. They ask themselves these questions:
- Who is the author?
- Where was it created?
- Who created it?
- What material was used to create it?
- How was the material presented?
- How close to the event was it created?

After asking these questions, historians can rank the source material from most reliable or trustworthy, to least reliable. The most reliable material is created at the time of the event by someone who either participated in the

◄ The North Atlantic Treaty was signed on April 4, 1949. The context of this cartoon by D. R. Fitzpatrick was the threat of the Soviet Union as felt by countries in Western Europe and North America.

EVIDENCE RECORD CARD

Cartoon: *Banner of the Non-Soviet Union*
LEVEL Primary source
MATERIAL Cartoon by D.R. Fitzpatrick
LOCATION United States
DATE 1948
SOURCE Topfoto

event or saw it happen. Next comes material created after the event by people who were involved or watched the event. Least reliable is material created many years after an event by people who used interviews or evidence to find their information.

Historians also think about the **context** of the sources. Context is the setting in which an event occurs. The common beliefs during the Cold War are reflected in the source material created in the different countries. The Cold War and the Cuban Missile Crisis came after the end of World War II. People were still suspicious and worried about the actions and plans of world leaders. In North America, citizens believed in **democracy**. This is a system where citizens can elect their leaders and determine the course of action of their government. Cuba was a **dictatorship**. It was ruled by an individual, Fidel Castro, who did not have to answer to the wants or demands of his people. When reading source material on the Cold War it is important to keep this context in mind.

▶ In February 1948 Soviet control spread to Czechoslovakia. The Soviet Union called it "Victorious February." This cartoon by D. R. Fitzpatrick shows how the West saw the events.

ANALYZE THIS

Study this political cartoon titled, *When the Time is Ripe*. What message is it trying to illustrate? Does it show bias? Explain why or why not.

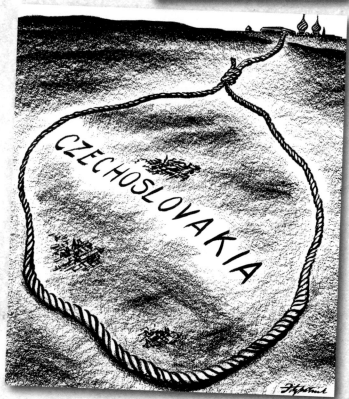

"President de Gaulle listened with obvious interest and then remarked that U.S. for first time felt itself threatened since missiles in Cuba were aimed at U.S. and they had no other reason to be in Cuba save threaten U.S. He continued that President Kennedy wishes to react, and to react now, and certainly France can have no objection to that since it is legal for a country to defend itself when it finds itself in danger."

Excerpt from a telegram to the Department of State from the American Embassy in France, October 22, 1962

THE COLD WAR

"The Cold War isn't thawing; it is burning with a deadly heat. Communism isn't sleeping; it is, as always, plotting, scheming, working, fighting."

Richard M. Nixon, American politician, 1964

The Cold War was a time of fear and tension around the world. It was a war of words, weapons, and technology waged by two very powerful countries: the United States and the Soviet Union (today known as Russia).

These two **superpowers** built up more and more nuclear weapons and pointed their nuclear missiles at each other. The world was still reeling from the death and destruction of World War II. People were very frightened that one wrong move would send the planet into another, even deadlier, war.

Things came to a head in the Caribbean island nation of Cuba. Its leader, Fidel Castro, was friendly with the Soviets. He allowed them to place nuclear missiles in his country. Cuba is only 90 miles (144 kilometers) from the coast of the United States. The Americans saw this as a threat of war and prepared to fight back. They sent ships to **blockade** the island.

For thirteen days the world held its breath as President Kennedy and Premier Khrushchev tried to find a peaceful solution. People watched on television and scanned newspapers for details.

After tense negotiations they reached an agreement. The Soviet Union removed its missiles from Cuba and the United States promised to not invade Cuba. The Cuban Missile Crisis was over, but the Cold War was not.

The two nations continued to develop new deadly bombs and missiles. They also competed to land a human on the moon. Through the Nuclear Arms Race and the Space Race, they pushed technology and science to new levels.

"All the News That's Fit to Print"

VOL. CXII .. No. 38,264.

© 1962 by The New York Ti
Times Square, New Yor

U.S. AND SO
KENNEDY
TO REMOV

DE GAULLE WINS 61% OF BALLOTS; ABSTENTIONS HIGH

46% of the Eligible Voters Support President's Plan on Choosing Successor

By ROBERT C. DOTY

Special to The New York Times

PARIS, Monday, Oct. 29— President de Gaulle won his referendum battle in nationwide balloting yesterday, but he suffered substantial losses of support in comparison with previous tests.

On the basis of complete unofficial returns early this morning, 61.76 per cent of the valid ballots cast were in favor of the President's proposal to elect his eventual successor by popular vote instead of by the limited college of 80,000 "notables" specified in the present Constitution.

But, with abstentions running at about 24 per cent of the electorate, General de Gaulle had only a minority— about 46 per cent — of the registered voters backing him.

Tally of Voting

Of 27,579,424 registered voters,
at 289,193 went to the polls and

DE GAULLE VOTES IN
de Gaulle casting ballot in

Castro Asks (
Strives to Re

By TAD
al to The N
Oct. 2
the Unit
ay. Thi

ERS
DLY

▲ Read the headlines: *The New York Times* reported the end of the Cuban Missile Crisis two days after Kennedy and Khrushchev had reached their historic agreement.

The New York Times.

LATE CITY EDITION

U. S. Weather Bureau Report (Page 57) forecasts:
Chance of rain, then cloudy today,
tonight. Chance of rain tomorrow.
Temp. range: 58—46; yesterday: 67—41.

NEW YORK, MONDAY, OCTOBER 29, 1962.

10 cents beyond 50-mile zone from New York City
except on Long Island. Higher in air delivery cities.

FIVE CENTS

OVIET REACH ACCORD ON CUBA;
ACCEPTS KHRUSHCHEV PLEDGE
E MISSILES UNDER U.N. WATCH

Associated Press Radiophoto
EFERENDUM: President
Colombey-les-deux-Eglises.

THANT SETS VISIT

He Will Go to Havana Tomorrow to Seek Castro Consent

Text of Thant note to Castro is printed on Page 18.

By THOMAS J. HAMILTON
Special to The New York Times

UNITED NATIONS, N.Y., Oct. 28—U Thant, the Acting Secretary General, will fly to Cuba Tuesday with his top assistants to discuss arrangements for a United Nations check on the dismantling of Soviet missiles and the halting of the building of bases.

Mr. Thant plans to stay in Cuba only long enough to obtain Premier Fidel Castro's acceptance of the Thant plan to send observer teams to inspect and be sure Premier Khrushchev's agreement to dismantle the missiles is complied with.

According to reliable sources, once the Acting Secretary General makes these arrangements, he will return to obtain authorization from the Security Council for the inspection program.

Mahmoud Riad of the United Arab Republic, who on day will take over the presidency of the Security cil from the Soviet delegate a talk with Mr. Thant. Mr. Riad said he saw nc for a Council meeting unt Thant returned—perhaps day or Friday.

Outcome Awaited

The Council suspended bate Thursday night to the outcome of message changed by President Ke and Premier Khrushchev. Premier Castro's conse

RUSSIAN ACCEDES

Tells President Work on Bases Is Halted —Invites Talks

Texts of Khrushchev notes to Kennedy and Thant, Page 16.

By SEYMOUR TOPPING
Special to The New York Times

MOSCOW, Oct. 28—Premier Khrushchev agreed today to end the construction of Soviet bases in Cuba and to dismantle Soviet rockets there, both under United Nations supervision.

In a message to President Kennedy, the Soviet leader said that he already had issued instructions for this and for crating and returning the rockets to the Soviet Union.

This was said to have been done in return for the commitments offered in a letter sent to Mr. Khrushchev yesterday by President Kennedy. The letter expressed the United States' readiness to lift the naval quarantine of Cuba and join with other nations of the West-

United Press International Telephoto
PRESIDENT ATTENDS MASS: Mr. Kennedy at St. Stephen's Roman Catholic Church in Washington yesterday before receiving Premier Khrushchev's message.

CAPITAL HOPEFUL

Plans to End Blockade as Soon as Moscow Lives Up to Vow

Texts of the Kennedy statement and message are on Page 16.

By E. W. KENWORTHY
Special to The New York Times

WASHINGTON, Oct. 28—President Kennedy and Premier Khrushchev reached apparent agreement today on a formula to end the crisis over Cuba and to begin talks on easing tensions in other areas.

Premier Khrushchev pledged the Soviet Union to stop work on its missile sites in Cuba, to dismantle the weapons and to crate them and take them home. All this would be done under verification of United Nations representatives.

President Kennedy, for his part, pledged the lifting of the Cuban arms blockade when the United Nations had taken the "necessary measures," and that the United States would not

uantanamo;
air Prestige

ZULC
York Times

— Premier Fidel Castro
States evacuate its naval
was taken here tonight as
major point in evidence
t Cuba's revolutionary
der was struggling to sal-
ge his prestige at home and
the rest of Latin America.
United States officials and
tin-American diplomats be-

ANALYZE THIS

An **accord** is an agreement that benefits both sides. Look at the headline of this *New York Times* newspaper. Does the headline give you the impression that both sides benefited? Do you think this is the same headline that would be used in a Soviet newspaper? Look at the titles of the articles next to the photo of Kennedy. Do they give you the impression that both sides benefited? Why or why not?

PERSPECTIVES

In modern times, many countries share borders and millions of people cross them each day. Have a close look at this picture of a border crossing between Russian and American zones in Austria after World War II. Do you think it was easy or hard to cross during this time? What details in the image support your answer?

POLITICAL DIFFERENCES

During World War II, the United States and the Soviet Union were **allies** against Germany. They worked together to defeat Hitler, but they did not entirely trust each other. When the war ended, they were the strongest nations left standing. They both moved to strengthen their positions in the world.

The two nations had very different views on systems of governments. The Soviet Union believed in **communism**.

YOU ARE NOW ENTERING THE AMERICAN ZONE

▶ Gates, fences, and guards marked border crossings between Communist countries and Western Europe.

EVIDENCE RECORD CARD

The separation of American and Soviet zones in Austria

LEVEL Primary source
MATERIAL Photograph
LOCATION Austrian border
DATE 1946–1949
SOURCE World History Archive/Topfoto

"From Stettin in the Baltic to Trieste in the Adriatic, an iron curtain has descended across the Continent."

Winston Churchill, former Prime Minister of Britain, March 5, 1946

The idea behind communism is that nothing is privately owned: Everything is owned by everyone. To achieve that, everyone must take part in making the items that are shared, whether on farms, in offices, or in factories. Prices of goods are fixed by the state. Everyone is thought to be equal, with no **social classes** separating people. The country's leader is appointed, not elected.

The United States, on the other hand, believed in **capitalism**. In this system, most companies and industries are privately owned. They are run in order to make money and hire employees to work for them. The price of goods and the cost of wages are kept in check by **competition** from other companies. The government is a democracy. That means that voters elect representatives to work on their behalf.

The Soviet Union decided that all the countries that they occupied after the war should also become communist. This included many eastern European countries such as Poland,

Romania, and Hungary. The United States was worried that the Soviet Union's leader, Joseph Stalin, would try to force communism on more and more countries, including the United States. The United States believed that **free markets** and capitalism were the best ways to rebuild Europe after the devastation of WWII. The United States stepped in to help countries, such as Greece and Turkey, stop the spread of communism across their borders. This was the beginning of the Cold War and it would last about 45 years.

▶ The Soviet Union used political cartoons to convince the public that it was more powerful than the United States.

WARS BY PROXY

As tensions rose, the two superpowers began fighting in **proxy wars**. A war by proxy is when two nations fight through other countries instead of attacking each other directly. How did they do that? If two other nations began a conflict, the superpowers would pick sides. They would each provide weapons, training, and other support to one side of the war.

The Iran Crisis was a conflict that developed just after World War II. The Allies, including the Soviet Union, occupied Iran during the war. They all agreed to **withdraw** when the war was over. Most Allies did leave in 1946 but the Soviets stayed. Iran split into two separate states with the fighting aided by Soviet weapons and military support and training. The United States protested to the United Nations. It put pressure on the Soviets to withdraw and allow the Iranian Army to return. Eventually the Soviets agreed and left. This is considered the first proxy war, where the Soviet Union and the United States did not directly fight each other. They used politics and pressure to demonstrate their power.

Historians can study the Iran Crisis and its role as the start of the Cold War in the primary sources that survive. These include letters, memorandums, and reports made by both the Soviets and the Americans.

The Korean War was also a proxy war. It started as a conflict between North and South Korea in 1950. The

◄ An American tank drives north through Chunchon, on the central front in Korea in March 1951. South Korea was officially supported by the United Nations but the vast majority of troops fighting there were from the United States.

North was backed by the Soviet Union and China. The South was supported by the United Nations, led by the United States. Neither side wanted to lose to the other. A victory in Korea would be **symbolic** to show one superpower was more powerful than the other. The war ended with a divided Korea. Primary source material for this important proxy war includes telegrams sent to the United States, reports from the military, and statements by President Truman.

▼ The movie and TV series *M*A*S*H* were set in a mobile army surgical hospital during the Korean conflict.

ANALYZE THIS

The film *M*A*S*H* was based on a book written by an army doctor who served in Korea. Is the film a primary source about the Korean War or a secondary source? Why?

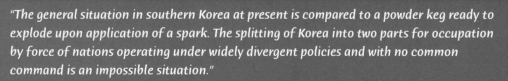

"*The general situation in southern Korea at present is compared to a powder keg ready to explode upon application of a spark. The splitting of Korea into two parts for occupation by force of nations operating under widely divergent policies and with no common command is an impossible situation.*"

Excerpt from a classified message from U.S. General Douglas MacArthur to the U.S. War Department, September 18, 1945

SUPERPOWER RIVALRY

The Cold War wasn't just about military strength. Each superpower nation also wanted to prove that it was the most advanced in science and technology. The two sides battled in two areas: the Nuclear Arms Race and the Space Race.

After World War II, both superpowers built up their **stockpile** of nuclear weapons. They both worked on developing a hydrogen bomb, which was even more powerful than the **atomic bombs** dropped on Japan at the end of World War II. By 1961 the two nations had enough firepower to destroy the entire world. If one attacked, the other would fire back and both would be destroyed. This was known as Mutual Assured Destruction (MAD). People hoped the knowledge that no one would survive, let alone win, such a war, would be enough to prevent either side from ever acting.

Fear of **radioactive fallout** from the use of nuclear weapons caused many people to build underground rooms, called fallout shelters, in their backyards. Governments

◀ The first test of an American hydrogen bomb took place in 1952 in the Pacific Ocean. Soon after, the head of the Soviet nuclear weapons program, Lavrentiy Beria, wrote a letter to Stalin. He urged Stalin to speed up the development of his own hydrogen bomb.

"First, that while we should not neglect our continental civil defense systems at present, it can be assumed that an attacking force if equipped with atomic and hydrogen bombs could bring about widespread destruction and possibly speedy victory."

John F. Kennedy, speaking to the American Legion, October 16, 1953

built them for officials. In Canada, shelters built for Prime Minister John Diefenbaker were nicknamed "Diefenbunkers." The building plans for fallout shelters are primary source materials.

THE SPACE RACE

The superpowers wanted to control more than the ground. They also wanted to control space. Each was trying to be the first to put a human both in space and on the moon. The Soviets built the world's first artificial satellite, *Sputnik*. Americans responded by creating the Distant Early Warning (DEW) Line. This was a system of radar stations in the north to detect Soviet bombers.

The Soviets were the first to put a man in space: Yuri Gagarin. The Americans were the first to walk on the moon, with Neil Armstrong and Buzz Aldrin taking the first steps. There is a wealth of primary sources relating to the Space Race. These include films and images from the moonwalk, rocks brought back by the astronauts, and also manuals, telegrams, and documents.

▼ Every year on April 12, Russia celebrates its space program with Cosmonautics Day. April 12, 1961 was the date that Yuri Gagarin circled the Earth in the first manned space flight.

ANALYZE THIS

What impression do you get of the Soviet space program from the details in this poster? What might an American poster of its space program look like?

THE CUBAN MISSILE CRISIS

The Cold War came to a head on the small island nation of Cuba. It was a showdown between the two superpowers. The world watched and worried as the two nations flexed their military muscles.

Cuba had been through a **revolution** and a change in government. Fidel Castro had taken the presidency from Fulgencio Batista in 1959. Batista had been supported by the United States. The United States did not have the same relationship with Castro. He ran the country as a dictatorship, which means the leader decides the laws without

▼ The United States cut off trade with Cuba in 1960. Castro turned to the Soviets for help. They traded their fuel for Cuba's sugar. This led to a close relationship between the two countries.

ANALYZE THIS

Why did Fidel Castro allow Cuba to become the center of the conflict between the United States and the Soviet Union?

"*Dear Comrade Khrushchev: Given the analysis of the situation and the reports which have reached us, [I] consider an attack to be almost imminent—within the next 24 to 72 hours. There are two possible variants: the first and most probable one is an air attack against certain objectives with the limited aim of destroying them; the second, and though less probable, still possible, is a full invasion.*"

Letter from Fidel Castro to Nikita Khrushchev, October 26, 1962

input from the citizens. The United States and Canada are democracies. In a democratic form of government, leaders are elected by the people, and the laws and actions of the government reflect the beliefs of the majority of its citizens.

Soon after Castro was in power, he formed ties with the Soviet Union. He also made changes to Cuban society by making it more like a communist system. The United States felt that Castro was a threat to the safety of the region and joined with anti-Castro Cubans to invade the country and overthrow Castro. This event was named the Bay of Pigs invasion after the inlet where the forces landed. Its failure was a massive embarrassment for the United States.

Castro grew closer to the Soviet Union. Fearing another attack by the Americans, Castro allowed the Soviets to place missiles in Cuba. An American spy plane noticed the missiles only 90 miles (144 kilometers) from Florida. The United States formed a blockade of ships to prevent more missiles from entering Cuba. This created a **standoff** between the Soviet Union and the United States.

The world waited and worried that this would escalate into a nuclear war. For 14 days Khrushchev and Kennedy tried to work out an agreement. On October 28, 1962, the two nations announced the end of the crisis.

ANALYZE THIS

Why would a photograph like this one provide evidence for the United States that their agreement with the Soviet Union was working?

▼ By November 1962, the Soviets had begun taking apart their missile sites in Cuba and removing the missiles.

VACATED LAUNCH POSITIONS

MISSILE-READY TENTS

THE END OF THE CRISIS

Not all the details of the agreement between the Soviet Union and the United States were public knowledge at first. News media reported that the Soviets were going to remove their missiles from Cuba. They also stated that in return the United States promised not to invade Cuba. Primary source documents that became available long after the event show another side to the deal that wasn't made public. The United States also agreed to remove its missiles from Turkey.

The end of the Cuban Missile Crisis was not the end of the Cold War. But the events of those two weeks had a big effect on the world. No one wanted the world to come that close to destroying itself ever again. Both leaders made speeches to the public to reassure them that they had avoided a nuclear war.

Transcripts of these speeches still exist. Aerial maps and photographs of Cuba proved to the Americans that the Soviets were keeping their end of the bargain. These images and other CIA documents are kept in the National Archives.

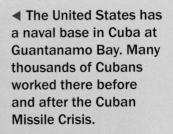

◀ The United States has a naval base in Cuba at Guantanamo Bay. Many thousands of Cubans worked there before and after the Cuban Missile Crisis.

Another important change that came out of the Cuban Missile Crisis is the way the two superpowers **communicate**. Information that is sent through other people can be misunderstood. The safest way to avoid any miscommunication which could accidentally lead to another situation like the Cuban Missile Crisis is for the leaders to communicate with each other directly. To do this, a "hotline" was set up creating a direct communication system from the office of the leader of the Soviet Union to the office of the president of the United States.

PERSPECTIVES

What do you think was Canada's perspective of the Cuban Missile Crisis?
Much of the country was also in the firing line of Soviet missiles based in Cuba. Did Diefenbaker agree with Kennedy's stance? See: www.usask.ca/diefenbaker/galleri es/virtual_exhibit/cuban_missile_ crisis/index.php

◀ Most people believe the Washington–Moscow hotline was a red telephone. In fact, a telephone was never used. The first hotline used teletype machines. In 1986 it switched to using fax machines. Today it uses a secure computer link and sends emails.

ANALYZE THIS

The American and Soviet governments exchanged communications equipment in order to set up the hotline between their two countries in 1963. How do you think each responded to this move?

"For use in time of emergency the Government of the United States of America and the Government of the Union of Soviet Socialist Republics have agreed to establish as soon as technically feasible a direct communications link between the two Governments."

Excerpt from the Hot Line Treaty, signed in Geneva on June 20, 1963

DIFFERENT VIEWS

"It was a perfectly beautiful night, as fall nights are in Washington. I walked out of the president's Oval Office, and as I walked out, I thought I might never live to see another Saturday night."

U.S. Secretary of Defense Robert S. McNamara, recalling the Cuban Missile Crisis, 1998

Going to war is never an easy decision. By looking at primary source material, we can see that during the Cuban Missile Crisis opinions were divided. Some believed that the United States should use its military strength to end the **dispute**. Some thought that the Soviet Union should stand its ground. Others thought the governments should find a peaceful solution.

Images of protestors around the world show how the public felt. One image from London, England, shows a sign in a crowd reading, "No War Over Cuba." In the Soviet Union they held signs of "Shame on U.S.A." Even in the United States people held signs that read, "President Kennedy Be Careful" and "Peace or Perish." The photos clearly show the feeling of many people, that war should be **avoided** at all costs.

Other sources show a different viewpoint. President Kennedy formed a committee to give him advice on the crisis. It was called ExComm, short for the Executive Committee of the National Security Council. Kennedy taped these meetings on hidden tape recorders. Transcripts of these tapes are important primary source material. They show that many military leaders wanted a military showdown starting with air strikes.

▶ Many Cubans fled Cuba during the revolution. They settled in the United States. These Cuban-Americans were calling for the Soviets to leave Cuba.

These Cuban-Americans are shown exercising their democratic right in the United States to protest the actions of Russia in Cuba. Do you think Cubans who were living in Cuba under Castro's dictatorship at that time were also holding protests in the streets? Why or why not? What would they protest about?

Signs in the photograph read:

Tanques Rusos desangran a los Cubanos

SIANS HOME

EVIDENCE RECORD CARD

Cubans protesting against Russians
LEVEL Primary source
MATERIAL Photograph
LOCATION United States
DATE 1962
SOURCE Topfoto

POINTS OF VIEW

Nowhere does the evidence show a bigger difference in point of view than between the two superpowers. Both leaders felt they were right in their actions. Both sides had public support. Both sides felt the problem lay with the other nation.

The Soviet Union was a communist state. It believed it was the only way a country should be run. The Soviet Union wanted to spread this social system not only to the countries it **liberated** in World War II but even farther. Posters were a way to share the beliefs of communism. Slogans encouraged the Russian people to work harder and faster to reach the goals of their country. These images also strengthened the idea for Russians that communism should be the system across the whole world.

After the crisis, the Soviet Union tried to brush off the importance of their missiles in Cuba. Source material includes an interview with Nikita Khrushchev's son, Sergei. He stated that the United States overreacted to the whole event. He believed that the United

▶ The fight for control of Berlin was a sign of the bigger fight between the Soviet Union and the United States. In 1948–1949 the Soviets tried to cut off supplies to West Berlin by closing roads into the city. The United States and the United Kingdom flew in food and fuel supplies by air to keep the people from starving.

States was used to being protected from its enemies by two oceans. In Europe, Sergei said, a country's enemies always have missiles near the gates.

The United States saw itself as the protector of the world's freedom. It would not stand by while countries were forced to accept a social system that they did not choose. It wanted to protect those countries which were trying to keep a capitalist social system.

Political cartoons, newspaper articles, and reports **portrayed** the Soviet Union as a bully trying to push its way into other countries. When the Soviet Union tried to cut off access to the German city of West Berlin, the United States organized an **airlift** of supplies to the people trapped there. There were many photographs and firsthand reports about this event, which served to reinforce the viewpoint of the United States about the danger posed by the Soviet Union.

▶ The United States felt that the Soviet Union was only pretending to be peaceful. It believed that underneath it had a dangerous military plan, like the dove costume on this tank.

ANALYZE THIS

Were the slogans, posters, and images effective in convincing each side of how right their cause was? How do you know?

"My fellow citizens, let no one doubt that this is a difficult and dangerous effort on which we have set out. No one can foresee precisely what course it will take or what costs and casualties will be incurred. Many months of sacrifice and self-discipline lie ahead—months in which both our patience and our will will be tested, months in which many threats and denunciations will keep us aware of our dangers. But the greatest danger of all would be to do nothing."
President Kennedy addressing the American people on television, October 22, 1962

PUBLIC VIEWS

Source material shows all points of view about the Cuban Missile Crisis. People living in Cuba saw events very differently from those living in the United States.

Cuban citizens living under the dictatorship of Fidel Castro would only be told what the government felt they needed to know. Billboards would reinforce the **ideals** of a communist society. Images of Castro were combined with slogans praising the revolution. After the Bay of Pigs invasion, a billboard near the site celebrated the defeat of the Americans.

Interviews with Cubans who lived through the Cuban Missile Crisis show that most people had no idea what was happening. Even the Cuban military didn't realize what was really happening until Soviet pilots showed up. Residents were told that the United States wanted to invade. They believed their government when it said that Soviets were there to protect them.

The public in the United States had more information. On October 22, 1962, President Kennedy **addressed** the people of the United States on television and told them the situation. This speech not only exists as a transcript, but a video is

▶ This symbol showed where a fallout shelter was located. Most were built for government or military officials. This sign was on a wall in New York City.

available online. In his speech, Kennedy told the public what actions the government was planning to take.

In response, the country prepared for nuclear war. School children began practicing duck-and-cover drills. Parents built fallout shelters in their backyards. Instruction booklets for these shelters, as well as information on stocking them, are some of the primary sources that exist from this time. Political cartoons and newspaper articles show that while most people rallied around the president's actions, some protested the actions of both nations which they feared would lead to nuclear war.

ANALYZE THIS

Do you think it would be better to be like the people of Cuba and not know of a serious danger so there is no panic? Or would it be better to be informed so you could prepare, like the people living in the United States?

▼ Instruction booklets listed the supplies that a family should pack into a fallout shelter. These included: tools, a two-week supply of food, a portable stove, a temporary toilet, medications, a first aid kit, an oil lamp, flashlights, and water.

HISTORY REPEATED

"The Cold War is over but Cold War thinking survives."

Joseph Rotblat, Polish physicist and
Nobel Peace Prize winner, 1995

The Cold War between the United States and the Soviet Union (now Russia) ended in 1991. The former Soviet Union broke apart, the Berlin Wall came down, Germany was reunited, and the former communist countries became democracies.

Some people say there is a new Cold War. New Russian leaders want to take back control of land they once ruled. This has created conflict between Russia and the North Atlantic Treaty Organization, or NATO—a group of countries including the United States that have banded together to protect one another.

Problems began as the country of Ukraine went through a revolution. The country struggled to set up a new government free from **corruption**. In this period of unrest, Russia, under President Vladimir Putin, invaded a part of Ukraine called the Crimea. The Russian military marched in, took control, and declared it a district of Russia.

Reporters say this new Cold War is similar to the old Cold War. Russia is claiming territories with force. It is also testing and moving missiles to strengthen its position. But there are also differences in this new conflict. Russia has more economic ties with the outside world than the Soviet Union did. This means that other countries have more influence on Russia's decisions because they can apply economic pressure.

In order to take action without public criticism, Russia closed down media outlets in the Crimea. That way it could control the information the public received. It could also spread stories that would help its cause and confuse its opponents. By hiding primary source information, Russia ensures that the public cannot make unbiased choices in elections.

ANALYZE THIS

Looking at this image of a U.S. fighter aircraft intercepting a Russian bomber in 2008, how has the world changed since the time of the Cuban Missile Crisis in terms of nuclear war? Are we in more or less danger now?

◀ An American fighter intercepts one of two Russian Tu-95 Bear long-range bombers as it approaches the aircraft carrier U.S.S. *Nimitz* south of Japan in February 2008.

NORTH KOREA

Korea was used for a proxy war during the last Cold War. But now that the active Korean War is over, the countries are still caught in a Cold War of their own.

North Korea is a dictatorship led by Kim Jong-un. It also has a communist-style social system. Like the Soviet Union, all industry, food production, healthcare, and education systems are owned and run by the state. In an attempt to control outside information from leaking in, the government of North Korea allows only state-run television stations and newspapers. This is to make sure that all information to the public agrees with government views. Posters and billboards repeat the messages the state wants to highlight. Some of these are: "Socialism leads the way!" and "Let's Make a Strong Grand Nation!" Many of these messages also call for North Korea to **reunite** with South Korea.

South Korea is supported by the United States. The United States provides South Korea with weapons, training, and **intelligence** for protection. South Korea is a capitalist society and a democracy. Like the Cold War between the superpowers, both sides in this standoff have access to nuclear weapons. There are threats and actions that keep bringing the two sides closer to an active conflict. In spite of worldwide anger, the North Koreans are performing tests of their nuclear weapons.

The difference between this Cold War and the past one is that it does not seem that North Korea is interested in avoiding conflict. The Soviet Union and the United States understood the reality of Mutual Assured Destruction. North and South Korea cannot seem to come to any agreement, even in peace talks that include the United States, Russia, China, and Japan.

▲ South Korean soldiers open the gate of a military guard area near the demilitarized zone (DMZ) , a strip of land that divides the two Koreas. Access across the zone is severely limited.

"If South Korea gets involved in the South China Sea flap, opposing China, then China will resume its relationship with North Korea. Right now that relationship is the coldest it has ever been. That is awesome. We really, really want this. The day China cuts off North Korea is the day the countdown to North Korea's implosion begins."

Robert E. Kelly in "Debating South Korea's Role in the South China Sea: North Korea Comes First," *Asian Security Blog.* July 30, 2015

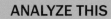

ANALYZE THIS

Compare these two more recent photographs with those of the Berlin Wall on page nine, and Cuban anti-war protestors on page 33. What do they tell us about the differences between the Cold War of the 1960s and present-day confrontations, particularly between North and South Korea?

▼ In March 2014 South Korean anti-war activists marched in protest against a joint operation by U.S. and South Korean marines. North Korea also objected to the operation, trading armed fire with South Korea across their disputed sea border.

STOP WAR EXERCISE!

TIMELINE

1945

May 1945 World War II ends in Europe

July 17, 1945 Start of Potsdam Conference where Truman, Stalin, and Churchill divide up Europe

August 6, 1945 United States drops the first atomic bomb on Hiroshima, Japan, ending the war in the Pacific

Jan. 1947 Communists seize power in Poland

April 1949 The North Atlantic Treaty Organization (NATO) is formed

Aug. 1949 The Soviet Union explodes its first atomic bomb

1950

June 25, 1950–July 27, 1953 The Korean War

November 1, 1952 The United States tests its first hydrogen bomb

November 5, 1955–April 30, 1975 The Vietnam War

October 4, 1957 The Space Race begins: Soviets launch the first man-made satellite, *Sputnik*

February 1959 Fidel Castro seizes power in Cuba

1960

April 17, 1961 The Bay of Pigs invasion of Cuba fails

August 13, 1961 East Germany begins to build the Berlin Wall

October 14-28, 1962 The Cuban Missile Crisis

October 14, 1962 A U.S. U-2 spy plane captures photographic evidence of missiles in Cuba

July 20, 1969 Neil Armstrong and Buzz Aldrin of the United States are the first men to walk on the moon

1970

September 1973 United States sends troops to help overthrow the government in Chile

April 30, 1975 South Vietnam falls to the communists

February 1976 Soviets and Cubans install communist government in Angola

December 1979 Soviet army invades Afghanistan

March 1985 Mikhail Gorbachev becomes leader of the Soviet Union

October 1989 Hungary declares a non-communist government

December 1989 The Berlin Wall is taken down

December 1991 The collapse of the Soviet Union ends the Cold War

For 2015 update: www.whitehouse.gov/issues/foreign-policy/cuba

1980

1990

▼ A map showing the target range of bombers and missiles based in Cuba.

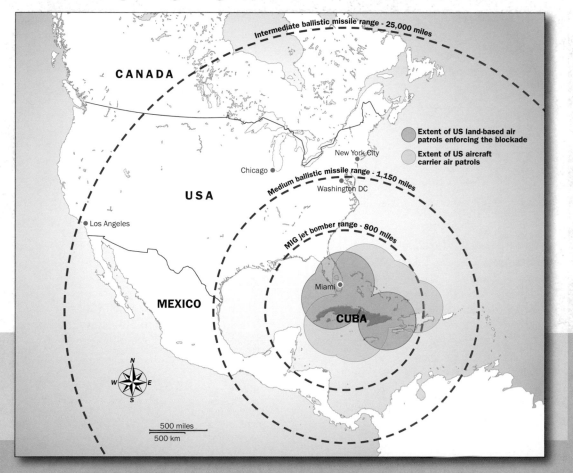

BIBLIOGRAPHY

QUOTATIONS AND INTERVIEWS

p.4 Søren Kierkegaard. *Journals IV A 164*, 1843.

p.6 Kennedy, John F. Address on the Cuban Crisis, October 22, 1962.

p. 8 Thomas Carlyle. *Critical and Miscellaneous Essays,* 1838.

p. 10 McNamara, Robert. Transcript of meeting on October 16, 1962. avalon.law.yale.edu/20th_century/msc_cuba018.asp

p. 14 Le Carré, John. *The Spy Who Came In From The Cold,* Penguin Canada, 2009.

p. 16 Cicero. *De Oratore* Book II; Chapter IX, section 36.

p. 18 Kennedy, John F. *Public Papers of the Presidents of the United States:* John F. Kennedy, 1962, pp. 806–809.

p. 20 Richard M. Nixon. "Cuba, Castro, and John F. Kennedy." Reader's Digest, November 1964.

p. 22 Churchill, Winston. Address at Westminster College, Fulton, Missouri, March 5, 1946.

p. 24 MacArthur, Douglas. Study collections: www.trumanlibrary.org/whistlestop/study_collections/korea/large/documents/pdfs/kr-6-15.pdf

p. 26 Kennedy, John F. Remarks at the American Legion National headquarters, October 16, 1953. www.jfklibrary.org/Research/Research-Aids/JFK-Speeches/Indianapolis-IN_19531016.aspx

p. 28 Castro, Fidel. Chairman Khrushchev's Letter to President Kennedy, October 23, 1962. John F. Kennedy Library and Museum, Boston, MA.

p. 30 "Memorandum of Understanding Between the United States of America and the Union of Soviet Socialist Republics Regarding the Establishment of a Direct Communications Link; June 20, 1963." Yale Law School, New Haven, CT.

p. 32 Robert S. McNamara. Cold War "MAD" episode 12, CNN 1998.

p. 34 Kennedy, John F. Address to the nation, October 22, 1962. Audio file: www.americanrhetoric.com/speeches/jfkcubanmissilecrisis.html

p. 38 Joseph Rotblat: Nobel acceptance speech, Nobel Peace Prize, 1995.

p. 40 Kelly, Robert E. "Debating South Korea's Role in the South China Sea: North Korea Comes First," *Asian Security Blog,* July 30, 2015.

INTERNET GUIDELINES

Finding good source material on the Internet can sometimes be a challenge. When analyzing how reliable the information is, consider these points:

- Who is the author of the page? Is it an expert in the field or a person who experienced the event?
- Is the site well-known and up to date? A page that has not been updated for several years probably has out-of-date information.
- Can you verify the facts with another site? Always double check information.

- Have you checked all possible sites? Don't just look on the first page a search engine provides. Remember to try government sites and research papers.
- Have you recorded website addresses and names? Keep this data so you can backtrack and verify the information you want to use.

TO FIND OUT MORE

Non-Fiction:

Bearce, Stephanie. *Top Secret Files The Cold War : Secrets, Special Missions, and Hidden Facts About the CIA, KGB, and MI6.* Prufrock Press, 2015.

Sheinkin, Steve. *Most Dangerous: Daniel Ellsberg and the Secret History of the Vietnam War.* Roaring Brook Press, 2015.

Sis, Peter. *The Wall: Growing Up Behind the Iron Curtain.* Farrar, Straus and Giroux, 2007.

Taylor, David. *The Cold War.* Heinemann, 2001.

Tunnell, Michael. *Candy Bomber.* Charlesbridge, 2010.

Warren, James. *Cold War.* Harper Teen, 1996.

Historical Fiction:

Almond, David. *The Fire-Eaters.* Yearling, 2005.

Cushman, Karen. *The Loud Silence of Francine Green.* Clarion Books, 2006.

Levine, Ellen. *Catch a Tiger by the Toe.* Viking Juvenile, 2005.

Strasser, Todd. *Fallout.* Candlewick, 2012.

Wiles, Deborah. *Countdown.* Scholastic, 2010.

Yelchin, Eugene. *Breaking Stalin's Nose.* Henry Holt and Co., 2011.

WEBSITES

A very comprehensive site from Ducksters including leader profiles and major events:
www.ducksters.com/history/cold_war/summary.php

The History Learning Site explores the Cold War with causes and a timeline:
www.historylearningsite.co.uk/modern-world-history-1918-to-1980/the-cold-war/what-was-the-cold-war/

Key events of the Cold War with links to major events from Factmonster:
www.factmonster.com/timelines/coldwar.html

Educational videos, lessons, and games from NeoK12:
www.neok12.com/Cold-War.htm

John F. Kennedy's address to the nation about the Nuclear Test Ban Treaty, 1963:
www.jfklibrary.org/Asset-Viewer/ZNOo49DpRUa-kMetjWmSyg.aspx

1960's vintage documentary Walt Builds a Family Fallout Shelter:
www.youtube.com/watch?v=OHmGn-oL2uU

GLOSSARY

accede To agree to a demand, request, or terms of a treaty

accord An agreement that benefits both sides of an dispute

accurate Correct in all details

addressed Spoke to in a formal manner

aerial Taken from up in the air

age A distinct period of history

airlift The transportation by aircraft of food, fuel, and other products to another city or country

allies Nations that have an agreement to support one another

analyzing Examining closely

archive A place that stores historical information about a location, a person, or an event

artifacts Objects made by human beings

atomic bombs Bombs that use nuclear power

auditory Related to the sense of hearing

avoided Stopped oneself from doing something

beliefs Things accepted as truths

bias Prejudice in favor of or against one thing, person, or group

Bias Rule A rule used by historians to assess bias in source material

blockade Sealing off a place to stop goods from entering or leaving

brittle Hard but easily broken

capitalism An economic and political system in which trade and industry are privately owned

century A period of 100 years

Cold War, the The worldwide political, economic, and military confrontation between the United States, the Soviet Union, and their allies that lasted from about 1946 to 1991

colored Influenced by something else

communicated Shared information or news

communism An economic and political system in which all property is owned by its members and is used for the good of all people

competition An event or contest in which people or organizations attempt to establish superiority over each other

context The setting in which an event occurs

corruption Dishonest behavior by those in power

culture The ideas, customs, and behavior of a people

decade A period of ten years

democracy A political system in which all adult citizens elect a government and representatives to govern them

dictatorship A political system in which all power is held by one unelected person, often ruling by force

digital Related to the use of computers and associated technologies; also referring to numerical calculations

dishonorable Shameful

dispute A conflict between two or more sides

document Something written or printed on paper

era A long period of history, with a distinct characteristic

escalate To increase quickly

evaluating Judging the value of something

file A collection of related government or other official papers

firsthand Taken from direct observation of an event

fragile Easily damaged or broken

free market An economic system in which prices for goods and services are freely set between buyers and sellers without intervention from the government or other outside authority

GLOSSARY

generation All the people born and living at the same time

historian A person who studies history

history Past events and their description

ideals Standards a society aims for

impact The strong effect on something

injustice Lack of fairness

intelligence Information gathered by spies

liberated Freed from enemy control

memoir A book written by someone about their own personal life and career

millennium A period of 1,000 years

Mutual Assured Destruction A system of military strategy and security in which the use of weapons of mass destruction by either side would lead to the complete destruction of both sides

nuclear weapons Bombs or missiles that use nuclear energy

outlets Publication and broadcast programs

pamphlet A small booklet

portrayed Shown in a certain way

preserved Keep something in its original form

primary source A firsthand account or direct evidence of an event

proxy war A war fought by two countries using other countries to do the fighting for them

radiation High-energy particles that can cause damage

recent Not long ago

reunite Bring together again

revolution To use force to overthrow a government

secondary source Material created by studying primary sources

secondhand Taken from someone or something that had no direct observation of an event

sensitive Very easily affected

social classes A division of people based on their wealth or status

society A group of people forming a single community with its own distinctive culture and institutions

source material Original document or other piece of evidence

spy A person employed by a government or other organization to secretely obtain information about an enemy or competitor

standoff A deadlock between two opponents

stockpile A large stock of weapons, materials, or other items, often for use in an emergency

superpower A nation with immense, worldwide, political, military, economic, and technological power

surveillance Information received by close observation

symbolic Representing something else

technology Machinery and equipment developed from scientific knowledge

tense Tight or rigid

Time and Place Rule A rule used by historians to assess how true and accurate a source may be

trail A series of papers, photographs, and other objects used to understand an event

transcripts Printed versions of something heard or spoken

treaty An agreement between two or more countries in agreement with one another

viewpoint A person's opinion or point of view

withdraw To remove or take away

INDEX

Aldrin, Buzz 27
anti-aircraft missiles 4–5
anti-Castro forces 16–170
artifacts 13
Armstrong, Neil 27
atomic weapons 26
auditory sources 13

Bay of Pigs invasion 29, 36
Batista, Fulgencio 28
Berlin airlift 11, 34, 16, 38
Berlin Wall 8–9
bias 16
Bias Rule 16
Bond, James 14

capitalism 23
Carlyle, Thomas 8
Castro, Fidel 19, 20,
    28–29, 36
Checkpoint Charlie 10–11
Churchill, Winston 22
Cicero 16
Cold War 20–31, 38
communism 23
context 19
Crimea, the 38
Cuba 19, 20, 28–31, 36
Cuban Missile Crisis 20,
    28–37
Czechoslovakia 19

De Gaulle, Charles 19
democracy 19
D.E.W. Line 27
dictatorship 19

East Berlin 10–11, 14
East Germany 14
ExComm 32

fallout shelters 36–37
Fitzpatrick, D.R. 11, 18, 19
Fleming, Ian 14

Gaddis, John Lewis 6
Gagarin, Yuri 27
Germany 8–9, 10–11, 14,
    16, 22, 34, 38
Guantanamo Bay 31

historians 6–7
history 4, 6–7
hotline, the 30–31
Hot Line Treaty 31

Iran 24

Jong-un, Kim 40

Kasimov 13
Kelly, Robert E. 40
Kennedy, John F. 6, 11, 26,
    29, 32, 35, 36–37
Khrushchev, Nikita 11,
    28–29, 34
Khrushchev, Sergei 34–35
Kierkegaard, Søren 4
Korea, North and South
24–25, 40
Korean War 24–25

Le Carré, John 14
Life magazine 15

MacArthur, Douglas 25
McNamara, Robert 11, 32
M*A*S*H 25
missiles 29–31
Mutual Assured Destruction
    (M.A.D.) 26, 40

NATO 18, 38
New York Times, The 7,
    20–21
Nixon, Richard M. 20
Nuclear Arms Race 26–27

primary sources 10–13
proxy wars 24–25
Putin, Vladimir 38

Rotblat, Joseph 40
Russia 38–39

secondary sources 14
source material 8
Soviet Union, the 20,
    22–32, 34–35, 40
Space Race 27
spies and spying 11, 14
Sputnik 7, 27
Stalin, Joseph 23

time, definitions of 5
Time and Place Rule 18
Tintin 14
Truman, Harry 25

Ukraine 38
United States, the 29,
    30–31, 32, 35, 36–37,
    40

visual sources 12–13

World War II 20, 22, 26